I'M THE ONE
WITH THE BLUE CAP ON

Jeffrey Knapp

I'M THE ONE WITH THE BLUE CAP ON
By Jeffrey Knapp
Book Copyright © 2011 by Dina Knapp

ISBN 978-0-9676748-9-6
Printed in the United States of America
First Edition

Published by Rock Press, Inc.
4611 South University Drive #450
Davie, FL 33328 USA
www.Rock-Press.com

Direct inquiries and/or orders to the above address.

All rights reserved. Except for use in a review, no portion of this book may be reproduced in any form or by any means, electronic or mechanical, including photocopying, recording, or by any information storage and retrieval system, without the express written permission of the publisher.

Edited by John Dufresne

Cover Design and Art: Manita Brug-Chmielenska Randy Burman, Dina Knapp, with Ruth Marten and William Blake
Layout: Melissa Macy

Publication of this book was made possible with the generous support of the Florida International University English Department, Jamie Sutton, Chair

Acknowledgements

Grateful acknowledgements are due to the editors of the following publications where some of these poems first appeared.

"The Acupuncture of Heaven" was first published as a chapbook by Do Something Press, 1989

"In Brine" appeared in Penny Poems Artist Against Racism and the War, 1968

"I'm So Happy" and "Pieces of a Map" appeared in *Poems and Photographs*, Plain Brown Wrapper Pamphlet, Emerson Review Press, Emerson College, 1971

"This Is a Poem About Killing Your Mother" appeared in *Ploughshares*, Winter, 1972

"Fernando: Life: Time" and "Untitled," appeared in *Having a Wonderful Time: an Anthology of South Florida Writers*, edited by Cynthia Chinelly, John Dufresne and Michael Hettich, Simon & Schuster, 1997

I'M THE ONE
WITH THE BLUE CAP ON

Jeffrey Knapp

VI

Table of Contents

Foreword, Micheal Hettich	1
The Acupuncture of Heaven	6
★	10
Apocalypse	11
Disorder; Vanishing Routine	12
In Brine	13
Prose Poem # 26	14
Spring Fever	16
A Lesson in American History	17
Memory: Chance	18
Post Card	19
My Morning Run	20
Satori in Diner	22
Sestina for Dina	23
The Dull, Dull Beating of Your Heart Heart Heart	25
The Foxtrot's Messenger	26
There We Were, Captivated in a Moment's Folly. We had come in the Search of Relics and Would Certainly Not Go Home Empty-handed	27
Too Many Feets Between the Sheets	28
You're Breaking Me Apart	29
Our Bauxite Face	30
Two Love Poems	31
This Is a Poem about Killing Your Mother	32
Warning	33
Sonnet for Washington	34
Rehearsal	35

Objective: Correlative	36
The Parrots of Miami	37
Ariel	39
Ariel Philome Knapp First Valentine's Day	40
The Sender is a Passenger on the Cruise Ship The Cologne-Dusseldorf	41
A Line of Turkey Buzzards Surveys I-95 But the Only Carrion It Finds Are the Dead Brain Cells of Memory	46
Alias an Afternoon at the Brooklyn Botanical Gardens	47
Even When Love Is Gone There Is American Express	48
Valentine's Day 1980 The Poem Grows Inside You	49
All the Stars I Wish Upon Turn Out to Be 747's Playing Tag	50
Love Poem	51
Miami Beach	52
1 May 1970	53
Song of the Egret	54
I'm So Happy	55
Eyelids Slanted Toward Morning	57
Fernando: Life: Time	59
Gravity	60
Far from the Transistors	61
All Night Long	62
I Scrawl Your Name	63
Pieces of a Map	64
Untitled	65
Afterword, Geoffrey Philp	67

Of Grace, and Taste, and Song
by
Michael Hettich

Reading these poems, many of which were written thirty and even forty years ago, I am filled with amazement at how vividly Jeffrey Knapp's presence, the tone of his sensibility and heart, sings through. I am filled as well with affection for this man, one of the most intensely-alive human beings I have ever met, a person whose energy could charge the very air he moved through, whose love and wit and sheer exuberance made all of us who knew him feel and think and *taste* more intensely when we were in his presence. In a time when poems—and lives—seem to have grown ever more constrained by bland conventions and safe forms of decorum, Jeffrey's richly-spiced lyrics sing like the gastronomic adventures he so loved. Each of these poems is flavorful and succulent, and the collection as a whole is a feast of pleasures and rare delights. This poetry has the savor of actual life.

    When my wife and I moved to Miami in 1981, there was a lively and wide-ranging poetry scene here, with regular open-mic poetry readings—at Books & Books, which had just opened, and at many other locations throughout the city, among them the North Miami Art Museum (before it became MOCA), and in restaurants and bars. Jeffrey was at the center of things then, a young man brimming with wit and intellect, dressed—like his wife Dina—with style, audacious style, which was something none of the other of us young poets could begin to match. With his caustic humor and amazing ability to compose "on the tongue," Jeffrey's power at a poetry reading was close to awesome. He would get up in front of an audience and just start riffing on what he'd eaten that day, what he'd seen in the paper, the run he'd taken that afternoon, and the conversation he'd had with Ariel the night before, when he'd put her to bed . . . and then miraculously he'd read a poem that fit exactly into his riff and led seamlessly into another. The poems themselves served almost as props in a performance of living theatre: When he finished reading a poem, he'd toss the page over his shoulder, look out at the audience, and perhaps start talking to someone out there, about their politics or the style of shirt they were wearing that evening—and then he was off again. I hated reading after him! And I think everyone else did too. The light and energy he brought to these performances just made everyone else's poems—as good as they might be—feel pedestrian and dull. And the poems themselves, those props in his performance, were completely their own, completely his.

Despite the grousing of some of the more curmudgeonly among us, Jeffrey took the craft of poetry quite seriously. But his was a particular approach to craft—hardly the careful "revise and then revise again" approach most of the rest of us practiced. In fact, I think he rarely wrote a poem more than once. He was deeply read in the poets he loved, and he could quote their lines and aesthetic arguments to devastating effect. He loved Pound and Ginsberg, Creeley, Anne Waldman, Ron Padget, Olson, and John Weiners, Patti Smith, Ed Sanders, Ted Berrigan, Alice Notley—poets of the open line, messy poets who wrote all over the page. He spoke of these people as though he knew them well. He disdained poets who took themselves—in his opinion—too seriously, as well as poets he judged as taking refuge in formal approaches because they had no ear—Joseph Brodsky, Donald Justice, Mark Strand, even Derek Walcott suffered his withering condemnatory wit. I think it's safe to say that he considered most poets working in traditional forms to be, by that very fact, nostalgic, taking refuge in preconceived forms rather than exploring the nature of poetic form itself. And he would argue with anyone about these things, irking most of us at some point or other for his outright dismissal of poets he thought inferior or overrated, poets whose range of feeling was too narrow for Jeffrey's hunger, poets he thought lacked wit or humor, or appetite. Since I admired many of the poets he loved, we spent many afternoons drinking coffee or wine and talking. These discussions often happened in the context of family, always the center of Jeffrey's life. I remember the parties he and Dina threw for Ariel—Jeffrey making individual pizzas, homemade dough and all, while Dina taught the twenty of so little guests to tie-dye tee shirts—while he and I talked poetry and listened to Talking Heads, or Philip Glass, or Laurie Anderson—or John Giorno, for that matter.

And I remember when our daughter Caitlin was born, Jeffrey was the first friend to come over—arriving when we were still bleary with joy and exhaustion. He wanted to hold her "fresh out of the oven." That was Jeffrey, to me: a poet whose true language was life itself.

Who touches this, touches a man. He loved Walt Whitman too.

One summer, when Jeffrey was adjuncting at University of Miami and I was about to enter the Ph.D. program there, he I worked together for EF Language school, housed then at the North Campus of Florida International University. Our job was to teach English to middle-aged professionals from Europe—mostly France and Italy—who lived in the FIU dorms for the month or so of their stay. Most of them had been promised quite a different setting than they found at FIU, to say the least. Neither Jeffrey nor I was trained in such teaching, but we made a valiant attempt, and we—and our students, most of whom spoke almost no English at all—had a wonderful time, since Jeffrey worked out a way for us to hold our "classes" at an outdoor restaurant on the Intracoastal waterway near FIU, where we spent the afternoons drinking wine with our students, reciting poetry in our various languages, discussing the nuances of

US culture, and learning about wine. Later that same summer, since we were both low on money and feeling adventurous, we decided it would be interesting to enroll in a research study being conducted by UM at Jackson Hospital. I remember being pumped up with buckets-full of glucose-sugar-water, learning we'd have to give a speech to a wall-sized mirror behind which (we were told) stood a group of psychologists with clipboards, while the electrodes that were taped all up and down our bodies monitored our responses. I was so scared and sugar-freaked, standing in my underpants next to Jeffrey, also in his underpants, that I could barely speak. Jeffrey, meanwhile, apparently unfazed, was talking to our reflections and to the invisible presences on the other side of the mirror, asking questions and commenting on their lab coats and hair styles—and on how well his underpants fit, how our naked bodies compared. He was always singing this kind of poetry.

As far as I know, Jeffrey was the first "Poet in the Schools" in Miami, and I'm certain he was the best. He had a beautiful way with children, a lovely gentleness, particularly in the classroom. He made his young students feel at ease with themselves, with their own rhythms of creativity. Part of his strength lay in the fact that he engaged them to think beyond "meaning"; he allowed them to be truly silly and thus comfortable in their own bodies and minds. He drove all over the county teaching poetry—not so much how to *write* poetry but how to inhabit poetry itself, how to live poetically as an act of resistance to all that is crabbed and closed, all that can be tested and charted. It is heartening to think of all the children he touched this way, the encouragement he gave them to keep color and imaginative wildness in their lives. I'm sure many of them still remember him.

It must have been in the mid-1980s when Jeffrey with a few other poets conceived of The Bicycle Poets, a project supported by Mary Luft's Tigertail Productions. Lincoln Road was still a motley collection of funky bars and interesting stores. Jeffrey would jump off his bike in front of a crowd of people strolling up the avenue, read a poem loudly and with great gusto and hop back on his bike. I came with him once, as a bicycle-poet-in-training. I whispered my poems and watched him, amazed, as he pulled scribbled sheets from his jacket pocket and read them while his audience looked at him in bafflement, annoyance, or with glimmers of delight. And then he hopped on his bike again, and rode off toward another cluster of human beings hungry for poetry, though they often didn't know it yet.

He had that kind of courage, that kind of audacity, that kind of wonderful, life-affirming heart.

THE ACUPUNCTURE OF HEAVEN

I.

Another one of those airplane visions. I'm sitting in the seat next to the engine and suddenly the window blows open. I'm sucked into the jet and instantly vaporize. It's a wonderful experience, joining the atmosphere. I consider the possibilities of individual cell consciousness, and at once I am almost everywhere. I atomize like urine from a space capsule. All over the world, I see R.V.s valiumizing Nature.

II.

My favorite part is when she listens to Cuban soap operas on the radio. All the "Como se llamas" and "oyes." We do not speak Spanish, but feel like we are at Palisades Amusement Park, and that is close enough. The screeching voices of women who always mourn fill the air. The gallop of horses who sound like they are in the refrigerator. Everyone in tight, dark pants, breathing in our air. The pulse of music slowly pushes into the room, like red blood cells in a clogged artery. It is a dream with no one dreaming it.

III.

There was something compelling about the manner in which she shook his hand. Her warm eyes alit on his, then darted off as if stung by an enormous courting yellow jacket. He tried to make a connection between this and an article he had read in *Cosmopolitan* on Body Language, but knew that the decorum of the moment had rendered this thought stillborn. His attention stuck, instead, on the single thread of shiny vermicelli that hovered near the ceiling, among the exotic birds and chirping insects that seemed a frozen memento to a previous tenant's acid jellified brain pan. The scene was set for love.

She seemed to smile. It was August, and the three witches who share one eye were talking to Perseus on a crazy television. A red wind blew through the room and knocked him off his feet.

"Are you going to sleep all night?" she said, waking him. A swell of floral music filled the room, and they kissed an everlasting kiss. Outside, fine birds sang a rocking cha-cha.

IV. (The Revenge of the System)

We were suffering from some kind of technical difficulty. We were making love, on auto-pilot, late into the night. At the penultimate moment, the moment when sea slugs and sprinters fuse into one frozen time zone, a bell rings, and a representative from the phone company enters our bedroom muttering something about long-distance calls from Iran. In the confusion, he melts into a collection agent from Mastercharge and repossesses our memories at dawn.

V.

They wanted to fight, strong and hard, to the death, had it been in other times, and would have, but at this point could not, for the life of them, remember why. They had trouble, for that matter, even remembering their names and, after often confusing each other with themselves, took the calling of the names of recent model automobiles, ex-wives, oven parts—anything that would give their mouths something to say. They had reached, quite pleasantly, that state of grace wherein immediately, everything took place in the past. They could not have been more pleased at the absolute nature their lives had taken on, nor more delighted that, for once, nothing will ever happen again.

VI. (Postcard from Pluto)

Two cars line up at the traffic light. The men in them are both listening to a song called "Zombi Love Darts" on the same radio station at the same time. They are in love with the same woman.

Around the corner, the cars line up as if to play a curious game of tug-of-war with the State Supreme Court Building. A man with a Band-Aid on his sweater is punching holes out of an ashtray held by a cowgirl in hotpants and a lasso.

The game goes on forever. A Gardol shield separates me from reality. Wish you were here where is the fucking beach?

VII. (It-Does-Not-Work-This-Time)

A dread saboteur infiltrates my life and makes me fight too much with my wife. I sit as still as an avocado seed, and suddenly every piece of furniture in our apartment pops into flames. It is too visually unreal and makes me wonder if the man who did special effects for *Apocalypse Now* had somehow gotten into our high-rise building. I think of the references in Irving Wallace's *Book of Lists* about people who have in whole or part spontaneously combusted. It does not work this time, this fighting with my wife diversion scheme. We cheer, instead, the couch and the rocking chair and scream words of love and tenderness through the fire. As our daughter opens the door to the room, it quickly and quietly vanishes. The air is staggering.

VIII.

A man and a woman are standing on a street corner discussing the influence of Culture on our forlorn society. They are in front of a Chinese restaurant, by a traffic light. One is wearing black, and one is wearing white. Having been conditioned by international Hopalong Cassidys and Roy Rogers, it is easy for us to choose sides.

One says: remember the time Lucy played a retired air traffic controller, dressed as Carmen Miranda, trapped inside a Reggae group on assignment from the C. I. A.? Now that's art.

The light changes, and as in real life, we pass.

IX.

Ignorance, pain, and human injustice . . . those times we hate ourselves most, realizing the inevitable pain we bring to other people's lives, no matter how close they are to our own. It is the shock revealed, knowing we have reached our own full potential, like opening the imaginary door to an imaginary room, and finding the horror too real to bear.

A feather detonates a skeletal tear in a poem.
Fires dance resplendently in the sink.
And the same pelicans float past my window.

> You follow the line of her
> Nose continues
> Until the Oh festering eyes
> Where hopeless birds fly
> And flowers fall out at night.

You should have known better.

APOCALYPSE

The teeth are the first to go.
Exudation fills the room
With an odor like snow.
Airplane wings fall everywhere.

The ears go now.
They sing the song
Of love they never knew,
As wildlife disappears outside.

A sudden concern
With living a normal life
Brings pus
To the thousand year old eye.

> How nice,
> This Apocalypse;
> We're given our choice of horses.

DISORDER; VANISHING ROUTINE

This, I thought
would be clear.
We go half way
and then
sit down with the morning
paper,
something
we do every day.
But, when the coffee
spills, it
surprises you.
it doesn't happen
that often.
Yesterday, I
didn't shit, but
wasn't surprised.
I hadn't eaten.
This, I
thought
would be
clear.
We go
half way, then
disappear.

IN BRINE

In the morning

        with we

                in our underwear,

                        we,

in the morning

And we

      now alone

            without underwear

                      in some love.

        In this sea.

PROSE POEM # 26

I shop for eyeglasses at the same optician as Daniel Ortega does. This time, though, he is incognito so as not to be recognized by the wispy couturier who has just followed him in from a boutique on the other end of the mall. He is speaking an impeccable dialect of German in a manner which suggests that perhaps his father was an immigrant from the Reich, like Mengele or Eichmann. But the subject of his discourse is "power walking." Power sharing. The tone of his voice is convincingly arrogant, and a small coterie of shoppers begins to assemble in front of the disposable-contact lens display.

Daniel's arms pump with such veracity and force as he extols the cardio-pulmonary benefits and the attendant anaerobic thought patterns which accompany him wherever he goes.

Your river is my piss, Daniel says, losing or finding his train of thought.

The ant crossing your lap is searching for the same truths you are.

The fox and the moth chase the same flame.

A small dog with teeth is more dangerous than a big dog with gums.

Never buy a horse with no legs.

Deep holes freeze faster than shallow ones.

Only the nouveau riche need to buy their antiques—the rest of us already have them.

Expect no gratitude from the wicked or the righteous.

A man who knows how to walk in the rain will not get wet.

The bone on the side of the road was once covered with flesh.

Fish live in water, but they are also cooked in it.

A mist of fireflies, guided by the light of their own eyes, fills the mall with an echoing song. Scabs fall off the wound of the afflicted. The international language of love, unmistakably dressed in Nike Air-Jordans, winks coyly as an optician falls to the floor.

And Daniel was just getting rolling.

SPRING FEVER

Summer light
Cozy room
And time
With no feet in its shoes

I'd love you if
And I'd love you even if
The cigar green bay
Burns

A LESSON IN AMERICAN HISTORY

"Miss Hearst was so frightened she wet her pants. The officers allowed her to change into another pair of slacks before they handcuffed her and took her to jail."
—Associated Press, 21 September, 1976

    Several handguns
    Semi-automatic rifles
    A Japanese-American female
    Whose parents
    Spent World War II
    In a concentration camp in California
    Where she was born
    Sawed-off shotguns
    The granddaughter of an American businessman
    Who falsified history
    A pipe bomb
    40 pounds of black powder
    And a cat, who
    like a horse after battle
    Must have felt lonely inside
    Seeing his friends go.

MEMORY: CHANCE

Memory entombed.
Quiet, senseless, without a care.
We put our hands on the door
And hesitate.

She thinks about the future: will she grow
Enormous, fat like the lady standing next to us?

I think about the past.
Will this time be different?

Together we equal the present.
The single act of
Pushing the door open,
The total crossroad
Of our lives.

Inside,
A supermarket.
What right did we have
       To expect anything more?

POST CARD

Dear Robert and Lorraine,

After writing a poem about
Presidential news conferences,
Here are some words I had left over:
> Table Manners, Chinese Miscarriages,
> Chlorine, Apostrophe,
> India Ink, Sports Cars,
> Weather Vane,
> Dorsal Fins, Vaginal Warts,
> Flogging and Narcotics,

> Stock Market, Dragon Mask,
> Angels on the Corner,
> Peculiar Personality Flaws,
> Schizophrenic Windburn, Pock-Marked Violins,
> Basic Structural Faults, The Man Who Bites Hands,
> Possible Worm Formations, Sinus Relief,

And Chicago, when it snows.

MY MORNING RUN

Someone is burning toast
Curtains of jasmine and oleander
Yield
As olfactory killer bees
Sting

Someone is flipping an egg:
Condemned;
And broken yellow
Stains the day

Someone's alarm clock goes off
Confusing one
Who thought it went
On

Someone falls out of bed
An axe falls in Tuscany
There is no relation
Between them

Someone is drinking coffee
Alone
In a dream
Waiting for the hot black bitter
To turn sweet

Someone rolls over
And blinks
At someone else,
The eye knowing full-well
What language can't express

SATORI IN DINER - OR:

Anything you'd want is:
Palm Trees in T-shirts
Alligators Taking Pills
A Box of Dressed-Up Alligators
White Birds Courting
Hey, Little Girl, Wanna Buy an Alligator
The Best-Dressed Alligator in Town
Locomotives & Alligators
Alligators & Tears
A Gas station in a Quiet Neighborhood on Pluto

(for Jay Taylor)

The waitress says to us: Sure!
I've got anything you want.
How funny we must look
Trying to be ourselves

Spending half a life
Searching for meaning
And the other half
Forgetting what the meaning is.

SESTINA FOR DINA

I feeling my bones a color television
Parked next to an illegal alien
Is this for what we have memory
Or is it the Rhyme of the Ancient Mariner
I must send them flowers
And let them feel the heat

In all of this heat
A sweltering television
Grows restless, as flowers
Plague the illegal aliens
Like the plague. The Rhyme of the Ancient Mariner
Eclipses Memory.

The memory
Of heat
Like the rhyme of the ancient mariner
On television,
Like the din of illegal aliens
Whispers carelessly to the flowers.

How she loved the fragile flowers
Entwining him in memory:
An ode to illegal aliens
Wrestling in the night heat
Nothing to pray to but television,
He dreams the rhyme of the Ancient Mariner

And dreams the Rhyme of the Ancient Mariner
Sailing in flowers
Fighting on TV
Rejecting memory
Only the thought of heat
Remains like an illegal alien

In the heart of the illegal alien.
The Rhyme of the Ancient Mariner
Like a dreamy leopard in heat
Embraces flames

In the memory
Of television.

In love, she is a flower.
He, a memory.
She, a television.

THE DULL, DULL BEATING OF YOUR HEART HEART HEART

The snake that binds your feet together
Is not the one you were born with.
It is, rather, the extended tragedy of
Living forever on a flat world.

The rapture of enlightened ecstasy
Knocks on your door like a country without mothers
The electric trains under the blanket
Give you away at night.

If I could find you in the long lost dream
Of silent storms and nightmare fragments
The executioner's smile would extend and groan
But it is long overdue.

THE FOXTROT'S MESSENGER

Pretend you see a man.
He's looking over your shoulder
While you're wishing he would not .

Pretend he touches you on the shoulder
And asks you to dance with him, go
For a ride, visit an airport,

Or more. Pretend
He speaks to you,
Whispers gently. Your eyes
Explode
Like amputated fingers.
Trains pass outside.

Say he takes you home.
The lights are on.
There is a picture
In the table, a picture made of glue.

     Hello!
I'm the one with the blue cap on.
I had to meet you, somehow.

THERE WE WERE, CAPTIVATED IN A MOMENT'S FOLLY. WE HAD COME IN THE SEARCH OF RELICS AND WOULD CERTAINLY NOT GO HOME EMPTY-HANDED

The old women on the beach blanket next to ours talk about Transcendental Meditation and their personal mantras:

"Mine cost me fifty dollars," one says. "That's nothing—mine cost me a hundred dollars!"

"I got the Hadassah Mantra."
"I got the Ben-Gurion."

"My mantra makes the sky light up brighter than the Bicentennial celebration in New York."

"My mantra brings Cary Grant back to life again between my legs."

The bones of the virgin rattled in her breath. They hung like frozen golf balls in the mid-air of solid waste. It was a foregone conclusion we would not leave with our own lives.

TOO MANY FEETS BETWEEN THE SHEETS

"He stuck his head beneath
      The green walls of night
And sent an arrow piercing
      To the chambers of her heart.

And there he . . ."

Forget it, Chuck.
I'm the bad dude
Who invented language
That disappears in a day.
People say I'm sly as a savage piece of glass,
As cunning as an ugly dog.

I kill flies
      from the wing up.

YOU'RE BREAKING ME APART

Be it not like you
To take an arm or a leg
But call me sweetheart
Screw me to the bed.

YOUR BAUXITE FACE

By the time you get this letter, I will be long, long gone.
The odor of mating jungle animals had proved
Too strong for even this old cow puncher.

The sun beats hot over the dense foliage.
An Oryx gently stares at me from behind a native
And I think of my insurance executive quietly necking with my wife.
Life is universal.

When I left Doreen's School for Animal Husbandry
I thought I had it over you.
Now your name beats in every tribal drum.
The heads on the Chieftains' wall
Make me cry for Walter and Linda and your bauxite face
But I will get over this soon.
How is Florence, my adopted niece?

TWO LOVE POEMS

In a quiet place
She removes the last
Trace of ever having known him.

He, in turn,
Quiet and dark,
Turns on his television
And tries to explain life
To his goldfish.

"Love always screws me up, too,"
the fish says.

Remarkable!

        It is someplace in New Jersey
        And she is sitting at home
        Watching Balzac on her Samurai T.V.

        It is in a bathtub.
        It is in the Snug Hug Motel
        And someone is shoving mud
        In the mouth of a fire escape.

        It is your eyes.
        They won't let me forget
        Anything.

THIS IS A POEM ABOUT KILLING YOUR MOTHER

Two girls knit sweaters
For Ricky Nelson.
He promises both of them
To wear the sweater on Monday
The whole time they are on camera
Rocky does not kiss either of the girls.
The blank look in his eyes
Makes you think that
He rips their insides apart
With ground glass
At night.
When Ricky leaves the Malt Shoppe,
You grab him by the balls
And run.
You want one of the girls
And he has two.
Ricky reminds you
That a major crime
Takes place in America every six seconds.
You wonder how he ever has time to practice his guitar.
Ricky explains to you
That he's
Just a horny kid and wants to get laid.
On Monday, both girls
Reveal themselves to be your mother.
You kill both of them.
This is a poem about killing your mother.

WARNING

Shot a man in New York City.
Blew his head off.
Hair all over the ceiling.
(Some way to paint a room.)

Tattooed that on my chest.
She just laughed.
Said she read the same thing
On a bar stool in Kansas.
Turn over and go to sleep, she said.

The woman drinks a lot.

SONNET FOR WASHINGTON

Tonight, George, as you sit a crumpled bill on the night table
Next to the Motel bed that shivers and shakes
When I put a quarter in the silver box, awake
Not wanting to be; as you watch me mumble
To the twelve-year-old ax-murderess who rumbles
Through the T.V. screen, shaking
On the bed with only one quarter left, raping
Myself, because I'm lonesome, and faithful, and humble;
As you catch the eye of an overweight farm girl,
Trapped inside the world's worst oil painting ever,
Whose fat blonde hair twirls
In the wind of a clicking air conditioner;
Witness, George, how life can stall
And tell my wife I'd never leave her.

REHEARSAL

Someone intercepts your glove hand.
You feel like Hart Crane
On the goddamn
Staten Island Ferry.

A dead gull, head submerged
In a bath of sunset,
Smiles, and turns into a shipwreck.

You throw your notebook off,
Aiming for where you imagine the propeller to be
And imagining you got off cheap this time.

OBJECTIVE: CORRELATIVE

Through the timid night
a fire burns
outside of no one's window.

The earth, unimpressed,
benignly neglects,
yet expects us
(if we read history right)
to somehow be different.

The flowers gloom their sultry nod.
The birds swift through untold air.
Cars avenge the loveless rancor.
Babies cry and thoughts are born,

Somewhere else.

It was February, the month of love. Fires were burning in unseen jungles. I closed my eyes and imagined mirrors on the ceiling of my bedroom and even imagined someone, an actual someone, reflected in them. I heard choral swells of music as I did the morning dishes in the evening of the morning after. I smelled I had never felt this way before, I thought, but I was certain I would soon return to a way I knew how to feel. How wrong I was.

THE PARROTS OF MIAMI

The parrots,
who go unseen in the green
afternoon shade, locked like oar-rests
in the mahogany-wood hammock
we walk upon,
bark like feathered dogs.

One moves.
The sound
breaks
and audible knives
cut the dusk
into . . .

they say they came from Parrot Jungle,
these mockers of the afternoon
whose red-tipped wings and
diligent-voiced breasts
awake even the white moon,
so subtle above us.

Or house pets, perhaps,
like the alligators of New York,
whose scaly nostrils breathe . . .
deep below the toilets
down which they were flushed.

ARIEL

Parrots in sunset
tonight you'll be
my sweet daughter's dreams

    A leaf falls
    and rivers and cities
    are trod on

Startles by the light
a quivering moth
echoes our night

ARIEL PHILOME KNAPP
FIRST VALENTINE'S DAY

The eyes fade
like a blue car
driven in the ocean
or the resonant bang
of a grand piano
just after

The eyes fade
blue in the night
like shadow's of a bird's wing
stuck in the eye of flight

The eyes fade
and open inward
dream inside you
seeing everything

THE SENDER IS A PASSENGER ON THE CRUISE SHIP THE COLOGNE-DUSSELDORF

(The following six untitled poems were typed together on white 5 x 6 inch stationary with "Rotterdam-Basel" and a sketch of a cruise ship embossed at the head and the following inscription across the bottom of each page: Der Absender ist Passagier auf einem Kabinenschiff der KOLN-DÜSSELDORFER)

Wild Rosie
beats her eggs
with cardboard
strips
of corrugated wood
and hand-me-down
paperclips
and razorblades
popcorn and raisins
and shoelace string.

****

our eyes followed
each other through the
snapdragon weed patch
& only knew each other
by the landscape

****

sister kate
goes down the street
with roads in her pocket
and birds on her feet

and passes mr. barney's Barnhouse
of candlestick wax and bubblegum blue
and eats off his front door

giving the backdoor to her brother

along the wood picket road
and white flowered bushes
listening to birds & trees
whistling in the afternoon

****

her eyes still smile of blue
her lips have not left mine
still we watch the stars move.
without lifting our heads.

the flowers have not gone from her face
the leaves now thank her with embraces
for the august summer's joy
and the sorrow of its passing.

bright petals reflect in her love.
a garden flourishes in her eyes
she stands in the fields of song
the sweetness of the fruits gives fragrance to the hills
she smiles and lights the morning

****

he
kinda said
something
and I
kinda
said
something else
and walked right into his dream
and he
kept dreaming the same thing
without looking around
to see if I was
watching the right things.
(if I was dreaming in color
—he said—
things would look very different—
and I agreed
with him
without letting him know it,
of course.)

****

1. once I heard a man
   listening to the Earth move
   under his feet.
   "Is it really moving," I asked.
   "No," he answered.

2. isn't it just like the night
   to make you think
   it's day?

3. Robbie & I watched a swift,
   brightly colored bird fly past us
   every day. It rose and flowed
   and flew by daily.
       Once we did not go out to
   see the bird pass and wondered
   all day if it was there.

4. We planted an apple seed under my window
   and watched it grow into a small wooden box
   and we sat on it and told each other stories
   of how it got there
   and how it should be removed
   after we leave
   if it were to last that long.
   the box became tall and slim
   and soon we were not able
   to tell it from among the other lines

that filled our sky from top to bottom.
As it widened
it took with it many days
and shadowed much of its surroundings
with all that it projected.
Its rainbow colored body
Often could not be seen
As it hid itself in the orange air;
Yet we always listened to its reed-like voice
Deceive us into thinking we were alone.
Soon after we would find it,
It would come apart
In unseen pieces
And become the two of us.

A LINE OF TURKEY BUZZARDS SURVEYS I-95 BUT THE ONLY CARRION IT FINDS ARE THE DEAD BRAIN CELLS OF MEMORY

(On the 45th Anniversary of the Bombing of Pearl Harbor)

A line of turkey buzzards surveys I-95
But the only carrion it finds are the dead brain cells of memory

I didn't know in 1961 that when Caro's Florist closed on Friday and reopened Monday as a fallout shelter store it was a metaphor

That memory on the 45th anniversary of the bombing of Pearl
      Harbor

seems as old as DNA

The lick of night puts memory to sleep for all but the largest
Buzzards, the ones who drive Mercedes under their own wings

Hitler drove a Mercedes, that's for sure,
Remember?

Memory sticks to you like scales to a fish
But the fishmonger's knife is sharp

And near

ALIAS AN AFTERNOON AT THE
BROOKLYN BOTANICAL GARDENS

A dead surfboard traverses
The mud-slung plains of Costa Rica
And stops at your door for some milk.

Five people get shot in a dream
And your husband tries to kill you with a fork.
All you can remember is your phone number and
How to tie your shoes.

She tells you it is all alias
An afternoon in someone's park,
But you know from her snowy saliva
It is how we tell our loves.

EVEN WHEN LOVE IS GONE THERE IS AMERICAN EXPRESS

When you are on vacation your money is not yours
And more often than not, neither is your body

As if to prove a point, the Angel of Death performs
A root canal on the hood of your Budget rent-a-car

While the Mormon Tabernacle Choir
Hums Handel's Messiah from the steeple of each church you pass

The erection in your hip pocket portends a satisfaction that
Even your travel agent wouldn't have imagined

You wonder whose idea is pain and whose idea is joy
But experience wanders like a roaming ghost

And lands in someone else's baggage
Which gets lost, of course, or stolen

VALENTINE'S DAY, 1980
THE POEM INSIDE YOU GROWS

This new life
Inside
Is something no poet
Anywhere, anytime
Could ever match in words.

No need trying
At last
The easiest poem in the world.

ALL THE STARS I WISH UPON TURN OUT TO BE 747'S PLAYING TAG

The dark tendrils of night,
Like a radioactive glue-sniffer,
Like an ocean in love,
Zoom to the foot of your door.

Wax is dripping
From the eye of a hyena
Asthmatics clutter the horizon with twenty-gun salutes
A rice paddy crash lands in an air raid shelter
There is a devil
                In my freezer.

LOVE POEM

From the incorrect beginning
Her two eyes became
The skeletons of two
Steamships in heat.
Love had visited this house before.

She had no trouble
Turning into
The belt around her neck.

MIAMI BEACH

In summer they graze
Sheep in swim-suits
Swagger like weeds.

In the summer they swell,
Bloated in the stenched air
Like dead fish
Washed to shore.

In the summer they sweat
And petrochemicals
Ooze from their pores
Like rabid leisure-suits
In heat.

In the summer they splash
And throw each other on the rocks
Tenderly
Playing their drama
To no audience at all.

1 MAY 1970

Call a block in New York City
Viet Nam

And have a basketball game
With burning children

While the father
Shoots his way to the office

At high noon.

SONG OF THE EGRET

I have seen the night winds dance a chilling dance.
Fascinating images commingle
With the sea grapes on the shore.
To hell with all this.

> Nuptial plumage falls
> In disappointed molting.
> So white and silky were
> The long tufts of breeding
> That looked so good in mating routing
> But now embellish hats.
>
> So much for this half of the year.
> I wanna strut,
> Push the cushion.
> Six months is an awfully long time to wait
> With nothing at all to think about.

The night winds dance a chilling dance.
A heron dive bombs a small fish.
Someone watches television in someone's ranch house.

So much for this generative universe.

I'M SO HAPPY

> *O Happy, happy liver*
> —Wordsworth

I'm so happy I think I'll
go bugger a negro dog.

I'm so happy I want to stop.

I'm so happy I'll tear these leaves
into pieces and no one will
know I've been here.

I'm so happy I think I'll
take my ears off.

Moreso I think I'll turn them into
a dining room chair and
hope they encourage emotion.
I think I'll let you sit on them.
It's about time.

I'm so happy I no longer hear foghorns.

I've given up stopping on ice.

I'm so happy I will call in-
formation for the number of my conscience.
There is no longer time to wait.

I'm so happy I will eliminate one city a day
Until I have entirely relocated the face of my body.

I'm so happy, I feel like a blizzard
left alone in your bloodstream
each snowflake a corpuscle
each cell a lover.

EYELIDS SLANTED TOWARDS MORNING

A Smith and Wesson hung by his side and misfired. He wondered whose idea of spring this was and why there was a mirror in front of him. There were words he knew he could use: Butter, Eggs, Milk; a woman moving her belongings from one window to another; trucks moving down the street. So much being filled with words and pictures. He was trying to figure this out, but turned from the mirror instead. A volcano of a smile broke all this. He was just beginning to understand something.

While making love with Robert, he sometimes becomes John, and John Edward, and Edward Robert. She thought she had a patent on this, but recently read in Shere Hite that she isn't. The Turtle-God becoming a Mid-East sheik, then John Lennon. Yassir Arafat. Dan Marino. Rats fucking in the stomach of her father's wife. A pork barrel of rats fucking. Rat traps going off. Then back into Mayor Koch. The tedium builds. A naked voice: Displacement figure—zero. Port side—thirteen. Smell of gas leaking—starboard. Smell of gas leaking—starboard. The bible at the side of the bed detonates, leaving precious little for Sunday morning breakfast.

Her eyes opened like a can of worms; dark boulders that smacked any remaining light out of the room. It was morning. It felt like a squadron of army ants had raced through the dawn and out the other end, leaving broken veins and cancer. She hummed. Someone was writing the alphabet. Someone was cutting out dolls in her lungs. She turns over and remembers what it was like waking up.

Her body presses snug against his: and almost wet contour, not unlike what he remembers most about his grandmother: plastic sheets with zippers, everything loose and hard. He felt like a cabin cruiser when she hit her private bull's eye. She cried; real tears; Goddam.

FERNANDO: LIFE: TIME

(For Fernando Garcia, who died of AIDS)

My daughter likes to say
That if our cat were a person
She'd be 95 years old!

If you were a cat,
Fernando,
You'd be 250

And if a lemur, 350
And if a platypus, 500
Or a bat, 2,475

But if you were a ray of light,
Fernando,
You'd be 264,410,536,100,000,000 miles

With galaxies between us just the same

GRAVITY

This is what
it is:
an apple falling
to ground,
our bodies flat
together;
a real sense of being.

FAR FROM THE TRANSISTORS

Far from the transistors of love affairs,
The lotions of excitement, the vehicles of despair
Far from the loops of time, the demolition squads,
The fictive gulls over harbor in song.

Far from the trade winds
And hands of dark alleys,
There is you:

> A jungle of fire-birds
> A snug harbor
> Between my eyelids
> And my eyes.

ALL NIGHT LONG

All night long
I sleep under
The grey starlight
Of a planetarium, trying

To relocate
The pale geography of Earth.

Spain, Jamaica, Saturn,
All in a night's work

And the gases of Venus
Are . . .

The Milky Way is
Your lips on my shoulder
As I sleep
Very far from here

I SCRAWL YOUR NAME

I scrawl your name in ground glass ripped from the heart of tree-frog
Your eyes float like popped balloons disposed beside the evaporated road
He signals the stars to rise and fall with each dampened sound
We nod, acquiesce, clouds in flight above time
You sent me flowers once, but they were dead meat in my hands
They went down for the third count, drowned in an ocean of pus

I pick your name like lice from hair
You throw your eyes like billiard balls on a green road
Her smile breaks even the whisper of dust
We nod, acquiesce, and rain dampens our bed
Your dreams call you long distance even when you're awake
They want it, want it bad, but you got none

I smile and your name writes itself like a rash on my skin
You float and throw it to the stars
It never happened before, you say, and I don't believe you
We fade, repose, and an ocean of nerve cells erases us.

PIECES OF A MAP

Thrown out of a space ship
a whole fucking frontier ahead of you.
You only get one. It is like
a galaxy of ocean bottoms turning the corner onto Main St.

      .   .   .

A book of poems
A book in one hand
One hand on your breast
Your breast in my mouth

      .   .   .

They have a ritual there.
It's called Sarah Coopersmith.
All night they talk about it.
In the morning they dance to it.
In the afternoon they leave it. It no longer can be used.

UNTITLED

I close my eyes and search for a theme
Reality, Death,
Love & Desire

I settle on, fashionably,
Crime in the streets
And search the beach-house for sidewalks and a subway

In the next room you're mad
Because it's a natural part of marriage
We must experience

And the dark ocean's waves
Wash out to sea the misdemeanors of my internal
Speech/thoughts without caring

Your leery gaze screams darkly through the door
And catches the attention of my Perry Mason
My Mod Squad, my Eliot Ness

So I go to the beach and battle a bottle for beauty
And watch a cockroach
Catch the flat falling of footsteps

And the eyes of palm trees
Pay me no more mind
Than a land crab

Whose eyes explode in the moonlight
In homage to the stars below me
Above me and on both sides

So I ask the moonlight on the wave top the meaning of Truth

And there is none, he said, so go home,
And apologize to your wife, and go to sleep.

Afterword
by
Geoffrey Philp

"What do you expect? I'm a deracinated Jew living on Miami Beach."
~ Jeffrey Knapp, circa 1990.

    The first time I met Jeffrey was in "gradual school," as he liked to call it, at the University of Miami. We were enrolled in a course on Irish literature and after class, we were introduced, I think, by Robert Ratner at a local bar. An instant friendship developed and even though we soon realized that in our practice of poetry we had differing aims, we shared a similar vision about the aesthetic principles, drawn largely from our reading of Ezra Pound, which would cement our relationship. For the next few years, however, Jeffrey was my mentor, an older brother, who introduced me to the literary/artistic life of Miami and guided me through the treacheries of graduate school.

    Jeffrey was brilliant and he knew it. Whenever he spoke in a graduate seminar, a hush came over the room. Even our professors were silent. Jeffrey's knowledge of literature, art, music, religion, and contemporary events fueled by his omnivorous reading habits, boundless curiosity, and formidable intelligence were well known. But it was his love for reggae and poetry that made our bond even closer.

    I like to think of myself as moderately informed about reggae. But Jeffrey knew some of the most intriguing reggae artistes such as Big Youth. He had even taken pictures with the legendary deejay who had released hits such as "S-90 Skank" and "Every Nigger is a Star." Jeffrey had also met Bob Marley, and his wife,

Dina, made a tam, which I believe was buried with Bob. Jeffery's knowledge of reggae was impressive, but his knowledge about music and pop culture was encyclopedic. During the eighties, a trip to Jeffrey's house could result in a pleasurable evening spent listening to music by Talking Heads or Joni Mitchell. It was one such occasion that I first heard about Patti Smith and was schooled by Jeffrey in the music of Bob Dylan.

And that was the essence of Jeffrey. He was always on the move, always sharing something new that he had found. These ranged from silk suits he had found at a bargain at Aventura Mall through the art of Purvis Young or Edouard Carrie-Duval to the poetry of Félix Morisseau-Leroy, for whom he translated many of the poems that were later published in *Haitiad and Oddities*. Jeffrey was always meeting new people and was generous with his friends, many of whom I now call my friends: John Dufresne, Lynne Barrett, Campbell McGrath, Michael Hettich, Mary Luft, Jan Sebon, and Adrian Castro—the latter two becoming part of our poetry troupe: *The Bicycle Poets*.

The Bicycle Poets was born in the studio of Mary Luft's TigerTail Productions. I had no part in the creation. I was merely a witness to the collaboration of Mary Luft and Jeffery working on a grant that would bring poetry to the children of Miami. For over twenty years Jeffrey, Adrian, Jan and I taught poetry workshops in cramped rooms in Liberty City and posh classrooms on Miami Beach. Jeffrey would always startle the children with the vivid imagery of his poems and his subtle confidence. The children were thrilled. Many of them were at the age when they were just beginning to develop their personalities and here was a man who was not afraid to be himself. In poems and in actions, Jeffrey conveyed the life-lesson that results from an artistic vocation: the discovery of one's self. He signaled authenticity in his words and deeds and this drew the children and adults to him. He was simply himself, and like his poems, which contained many of the contradictions of his life, he resolved them in Pound's dictum: "Make it new."

This was Jeffrey credo. Coming back to these poems, many of which I heard for the first time when we gave performances in Miami-Dade, Broward, and Monroe counties during the eighties and nineties, I am still amazed at Jeffrey's ability to create memorable lines and the sometimes savage wit that he displayed in "Prose Poem #26" where he eviscerates the banality of evil in the personage of Daniel Ortega. Or the mindless materialism in "Even When Love is Gone There is American Express." This is countered by the gentleness of "Ariel Philome Knapp First Valentine's Day." What informs many of Jeffrey's poems is a sense of the absurd drawn from the Dadaists, Modernist avant-garde art, and the wittings of William Blake, William Butler Yeats, Samuel Becket, Jean Paul Sartre, Albert Camus, and Hart Crane, to name a few. He then, grounds his poem in landscapes from New Jersey through Boston and down to Miami Beach, with sensory images that reinforce the intellectual underpinning of the poems.

"Anything you say about Miami, the opposite is also true." Miami had become Jeffrey's home where he would settle with Dina and their two children, Astra and Ariel. It is also, where he would write fine poems about his love for them and this thin sliver of land buffeted on either side by the sea. Reading this collection, you will encounter some of the passion, intelligence, vigor, curiosity and the grace of Jeffrey's life in poems that challenge and charm. Yet you will experience only a small fraction of the man, who despite his conscious knowledge of his and our fragility was so willing to love. I wish you could have known him.

www.ingramcontent.com/pod-product-compliance
Lightning Source LLC
Chambersburg PA
CBHW031211090426
42736CB00009B/867